Sun

William B

Consultant

JoBea Holt, Ph.D.
The Climate Project
Nashville, Tennessee

Publishing Credits

Dona Herweck Rice, *Editor-in-Chief*; Lee Aucoin, *Creative Director*; Don Tran, *Print Production Manager*; Timothy J. Bradley, *Illustration Manager*; Chris McIntyre, *Editorial Director*; James Anderson, *Associate Editor*; Jamey Acosta, *Associate Editor*; Jane Gould, *Editor*; Peter Balaskas, *Editorial Administrator*; Neri Garcia, *Senior Designer*; Stephanie Reid, *Photo Editor*; Rachelle Cracchiolo, M.S.Ed., *Publisher*

Image Credits

Teacher Created Materials

5301 Oceanus Drive
Huntington Beach, CA 92649-1030
http://www.tcmpub.com

ISBN 978-1-4333-1426-1

©2011 Teacher Created Materials, Inc.

Table of Contents

Twinkle, Twinkle, Little Sun

Our sun is very important. It gives us the light and heat we need to live.

That is because the sun is really a **star**!

The sun is the nearest star to Earth.

The sun is a huge ball of hot **gas**. The gas is burning. That is why the sun is so hot and bright. It is like a big ball of fire!

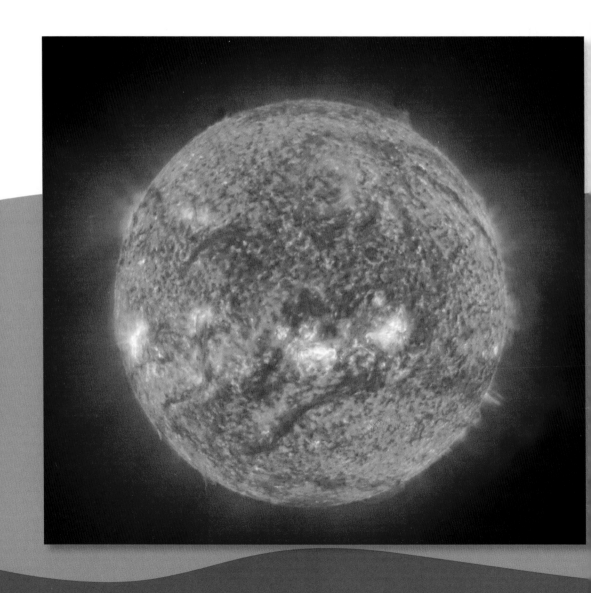

Living things on Earth use the sun's light and heat.

The sun shoots out loops of hot gas, too. It would not be safe to get too close to the sun!

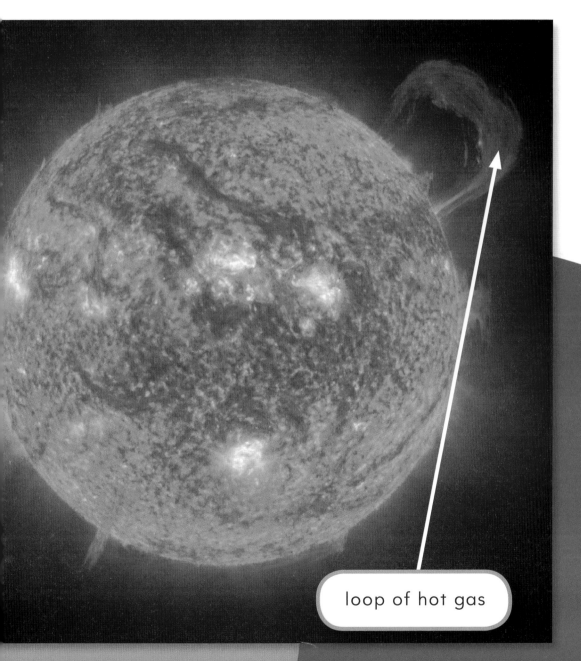

loop of hot gas

A Sunny Universe

There are many stars shining in space. Some stars have **planets** that move around them. The sun is one of those stars.

Mercury

Jupiter

sun

Venus

Earth

Mars

Saturn

Neptune

Uranus

The planets move in space around the sun.

All of space is called the **universe**. There are many stars like the sun in the universe. The sun is the star that is closest to Earth.

Our sun is one of many stars in the Milky Way galaxy.

The Universe

What is the universe? It is everything everywhere. The universe is made of stars, planets, and everything in space.

Stars are very old. The sun is about five **billion** years old!

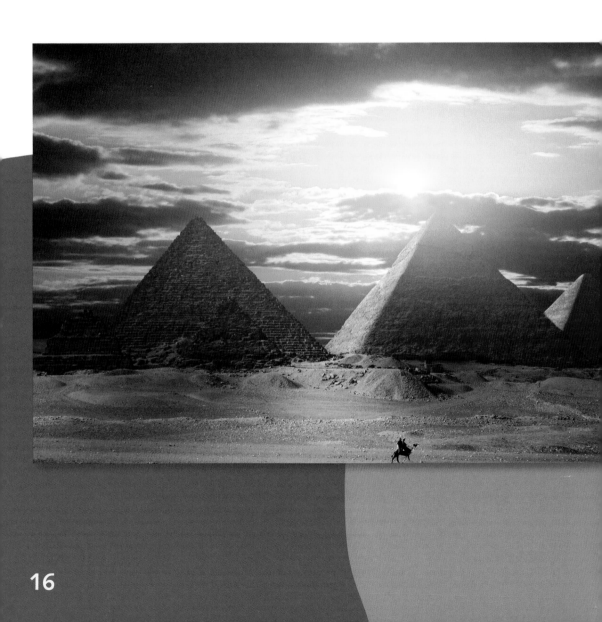

Big telescopes like this make seeing faraway stars much easier.

Stars are also very big. The sun is huge! Earth is like a tiny dot next to the sun. It would take more than one **million** Earths to fill up the sun.

sun

Earth

Sun Facts

The sun is made of six layers. The middle layer is the **core**. The core is the hottest layer. The outside layer is the **corona**. We see the corona from Earth.

the sun's corona

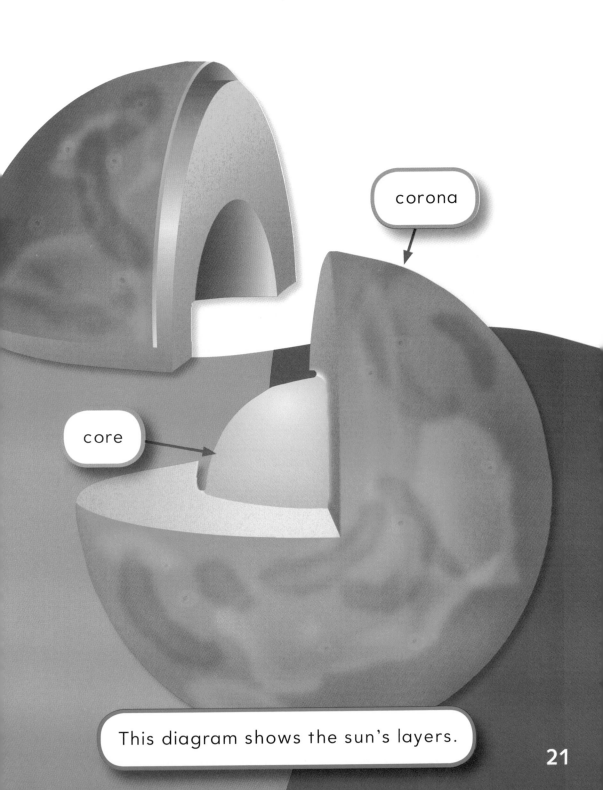

corona

core

This diagram shows the sun's layers.

The sun can be seen from Earth every day. But the sun does not move. Earth moves around the sun.

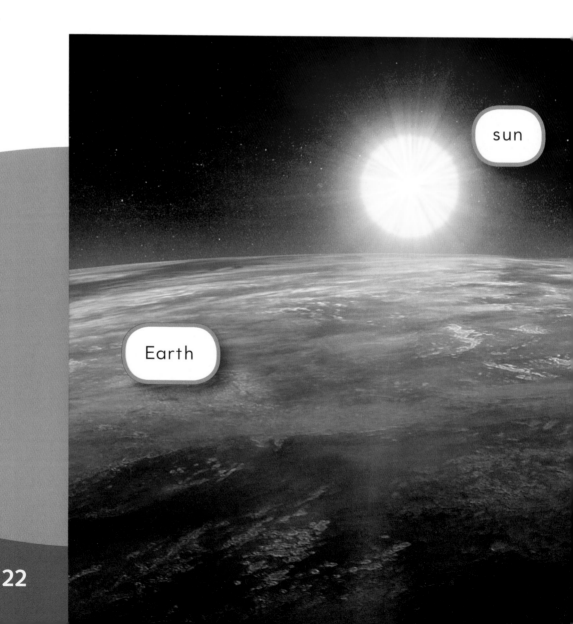

sun

Earth

Earth also spins. The spinning Earth makes day and night. It is day when a part of Earth faces the sun. It is night when that part faces away from the sun.

day

night

Each day, the sun seems to rise in the east. That makes the sunrise. Each night, it seems to set in the west. That makes the sunset.

sunrise

It starts all over again the next day!

sunset

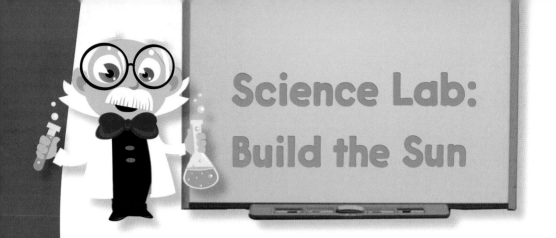

Science Lab: Build the Sun

You can build a model of the special star, our sun, with all six of its layers.

Materials:

- an apple
- four colors of modeling clay
- yellow or orange tissue paper
- tape or glue
- craft knife (for grown-ups only!)

Procedure:

1. Hold the apple. That will be the sun's core. The **core** is the first layer of the sun.

2. Choose one clay color. Mold it around the apple. It should be about as thick as the apple. That will be the second layer of the sun.

3. Choose another color. Mold it around the last layer. It should be about half as thick. That is the third layer of the sun.

4. Choose another color. Mold it. It should be very thin. That is the fourth layer of the sun.

5. Choose the last color. Mold it. It should be very thin. That is the fifth layer of the sun.

6. Crinkle up the tissue paper. Tape or glue it around the model. That is the **corona**. It is the sixth layer.

7. Have a grown-up cut the model in half. Now you can see all the layers that make the sun.

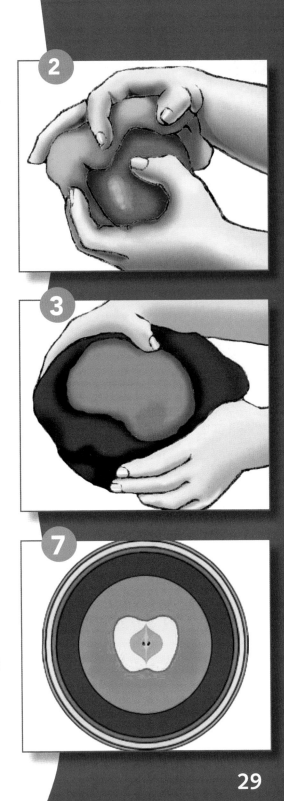

Glossary

billion—one thousand millions; 1,000,000,000

core—the inner layer of the sun

corona—the outer layer of the sun

gas—a state of matter that is not liquid or solid

million—one thousand thousands; 1,000,000

planets—objects in space that move around the sun or another star

star—big ball of burning gas in space

universe—everything in space

Index

A Scientist Today

Sallie Baliunas is a scientist who studies stars. She likes to learn about stars, like Earth's sun, that have their own planets. She has won a lot of awards for her work.